Mary

God's Masterpiece

1955

JOHN J. CRAWLEY & CO., INC.

NEW YORK

IMPRIMI POTEST

JOHN SEPHTON, C.SS.R.

PROVINCIAL SUPERIOR

DECEMBER 8, 1953, FEAST OF THE IMMACULATE CONCEPTION
AND BEGINNING OF THE MARIAN YEAR.

IMPRIMATUR

FRANCIS CARDINAL SPELLMAN

ARCHBISHOP OF NEW YORK

FEBRUARY 12, 1954, FEAST OF OUR LADY OF LOURDES

TEXT TAKEN FROM
THE CONFRATERNITY OF CHRISTIAN DOCTRINE EDITION
OF THE HOLY BIBLE
THE DAILY MISSAL AND THE ROMAN BREVIARY

LITHOGRAPHED IN U.S.A.

Dedication

The Redemptorists lovingly dedicate this little book to our Blessed Lady under her chosen title of PERPETUAL HELP. As sons of St. Alphonsus Maria Liguori, one of the foremost champions of the Immaculate Conception, they offer this humble tribute to

MARY

GOD'S MASTERPIECE

May this Madonna from the East, so ardently received and cherished by the nations of the West, be a lasting bond between them! May this Marian link help to bring about the much desired union of the separated Oriental Churches with that of Rome!

MADRID, PRADO   BARTOLOMÉ MURILLO, 1617-1682

THE IMMACULATE CONCEPTION

Mother Most Pure, Pray for Us

T HE radiant crown of glory, with which
the most pure brow of the Virgin Mother was encircled
by God, seems to Us to shine more brilliantly, as We
recall to mind the day, on which, one hundred years
ago, Our Predecessor of happy memory Pius IX, sur-
rounded by a vast retinue of Cardinals and Bishops,
with infallible apostolic authority defined, pronounced
and solemnly sanctioned "that the doctrine, which
holds that the Most Blessed Virgin Mary at the first
moment of her conception was, by singular grace and
privilege of the Omnipotent God, in virtue of the
merits of Jesus Christ, Saviour of the Human race,
preserved from all stains of original sin, is revealed by
God, and therefore to be firmly and resolutely believed
by all the faithful."

ENCYCLICAL OF HIS HOLINESS POPE PIUS XII

5

Now the origin of Christ was in this wise. When Mary his mother had been betrothed to Joseph, before they came together, she was found to be with child by the Holy Spirit. But Joseph her husband, being a just man, and not wishing to expose her to reproach, was minded to put her away privately. But while he thought on these things, behold, an angel of the Lord appeared to him in a dream, saying, "Do not be afraid, Joseph, son of David, to take to thee Mary thy wife, for that which is begotten in her is of the Holy Spirit. And she shall bring forth a son, and thou shalt call his name Jesus. . . ."

MATTHEW 1, 18-21

. . . A VIRGIN betrothed to a man named Joseph, of the house of David, and the virgin's name was Mary.

LUKE 1, 27

I WILL greatly rejoice in the Lord, and my soul shall be joyful in my God. For he hath clothed me with the garments of salvation; and with the robe of justice he hath covered me, as a bridegroom decked with a crown, and as a bride adorned with her jewels.

ISAIAS 61, 10

THE ESPOUSALS OF THE VIRGIN

Virgin Most Faithful, Pray for Us

7

FOR thou art happy, O holy Virgin Mary, and most worthy of all praise: because from thee arose the sun of justice, Christ our Lord.

OFFERTORY: II MASS OF THE BLESSED VIRGIN

NOW in the sixth month the angel Gabriel was sent forth from God to a town of Galilee called Nazareth, to a virgin betrothed to a man named Joseph, of the house of David, and the virgin's name was Mary. And when the angel had come to her, he said, "Hail, full of grace, the Lord is with thee. Blessed art thou among women." When she had heard him she was troubled at his word, and kept pondering what manner of greeting this might be.

And the angel said to her, "Do not be afraid, Mary, for thou hast found grace with God. Behold, thou shalt conceive in thy womb and shalt bring forth a son; and thou shalt call his name Jesus. He shall be great, and shall be called the Son of the Most High; and the Lord God will give him the throne of David his father, and he shall be king over the house of Jacob forever; and of his kingdom there shall be no end."

LUKE 1, 26-33

. . . BEHOLD a virgin shall conceive, and bear a son, and his name shall be called Emmanuel.

ISAIAS 7, 14

NEW YORK
METROPOLITAN MUSEUM OF ART

ATTR. TO JAN VAN EYCK,
1370?-1440?

THE ANNUNCIATION

Mother of Divine Grace, Pray for Us

9

Now in those days Mary arose and went with haste into the hill country, to a town of Juda. And she entered the house of Zachary and saluted Elizabeth. And it came to pass, when Elizabeth heard the greeting of Mary, that the babe in her womb leapt. And Elizabeth was filled with the Holy Spirit, and cried out with a loud voice, saying, "Blessed art thou among women and blessed is the fruit of thy womb! And how have I deserved that the mother of my Lord should come to me?"

LUKE 1, 39-43

And Mary said,
"My soul magnifies the Lord, and my spirit rejoices in God my Savior;

Because he has regarded the lowliness of his handmaid; for, behold, henceforth all generations shall call me blessed;

Because he who is mighty has done great things for me, and holy is his name;

And his mercy is from generation to generation on those who fear him.

He has shown might with his arm, he has scattered the proud in the conceit of their heart.

He has put down the mighty from their thrones, and has exalted the lowly.

He has filled the hungry with good things, and the rich he has sent away empty.

He has given help to Israel, his servant, mindful of his mercy.

Even as he spoke to our fathers: to Abraham and to his posterity forever."

LUKE 1, 46-55

DOMENICO GHIRLANDAIO, 1449-1494

THE VISITATION

Cause of Our Joy, Pray for Us

"BEHOLD, the virgin shall be with child, and shall bring forth a son; and they shall call his name Emmanuel"; which is, interpreted, "God with us."

MATTHEW 1, 23

NOW it came to pass in those days, that a decree went forth from Cæsar Augustus that a census of the whole world should be taken. This first census took place while Cyrinus was governor of Syria. And all were going, each to his own town, to register.

And Joseph also went from Galilee out of the town of Nazareth into Judea to the town of David, which is called Bethlehem—because he was of the house and family of David—to register, together with Mary his espoused wife, who was with child. And it came to pass while they were there, that the days for her to be delivered were fulfilled. And she brought forth her firstborn son, and wrapped him in swaddling clothes, and laid him in a manger, because there was no room for them in the inn.

LUKE 2, 1-7

IN the beginning was the Word, and the Word was with God; and the Word was God . . . And the Word was made flesh, and dwelt among us. And we saw his glory . . .

JOHN 1, 1 AND 14

12

THE NATIVITY

Mother of Christ, Pray for Us

ND there were shepherds in the same district living in the fields and keeping watch over their flock by night. And behold, an angel of the Lord stood by them and the glory of God shone round about them, and they feared exceedingly. And the angel said to them, "Do not be afraid, for behold, I bring you good news of great joy which shall be to all the people; for today in the town of David a Savior has been born to you, who is Christ the Lord. And this shall be a sign to you: you will find an infant wrapped in swaddling clothes and lying in a manger." And suddenly there was with the angel a multitude of the heavenly host praising God and saying, "Glory to God in the highest, and on earth peace among men of good will."

And it came to pass, when the angels had departed from them into heaven, that the shepherds were saying to one another, "Let us go over to Bethlehem and see this thing that has come to pass, which the Lord has made known to us." So they went with haste, and they found Mary and Joseph, and the babe lying in the manger. And when they had seen, they understood what had been told them concerning this child. And all who heard marvelled at the things told them by the shepherds. But Mary kept in mind all these things, pondering them in her heart. And the shepherds returned, glorifying and praising God for all that they had heard and seen, even as it was spoken to them.

LUKE 2, 8-20

14

FLORENCE, UFFIZI GALLERY   GHERARDO DELLA NOTTE,
                                        1590-1656

THE ADORATION OF THE SHEPHERDS

Mother of Our Savior, Pray for Us

Now when Jesus was born in Bethlehem of Judea, in the days of King Herod, behold, Magi came from the East to Jerusalem, saying, "Where is he that is born king of the Jews? For we have seen his star in the East and have come to worship him." But when King Herod heard this, he was troubled, and so was all Jerusalem with him. And gathering together all the chief priests and Scribes of the people, he inquired of them where the Christ was to be born. And they said to him, "In Bethlehem of Judea; for thus it is written by the prophet, 'And thou, Bethlehem, of the land of Juda, art by no means least among the princes of Juda; for from thee shall come forth a leader who shall rule my people Israel.' "

Then Herod summoned the Magi secretly, and carefully ascertained from them the time when the star had appeared to them. And sending them to Bethlehem, he said, "Go and make careful inquiry concerning the child, and when you have found him, bring me word, that I too may go and worship him." Now they, having heard the king, went their way. And behold, the star that they had seen in the East went before them, until it came and stood over the place where the child was. And when they saw the star they rejoiced exceedingly. And entering the house, they found the child with Mary his mother, and falling down they worshipped him. And opening their treasures they offered him gifts of gold, frankincense and myrrh. And being warned in a dream not to return to Herod, they went back to their own country by another way.

MATTHEW 2, 1-12

PARIS, THE LOUVRE   BERNARDINO LUINI, c.1475-1532

THE ADORATION OF THE KINGS

Morning Star, Pray for Us

17

And when the days of her purification were fulfilled according to the Law of Moses, they took him up to Jerusalem to present him to the Lord— as it is written in the Law of the Lord, "Every male that opens the womb shall be called holy to the Lord" —and to offer a sacrifice according to what is said in the Law of the Lord, "a pair of turtledoves or two young pigeons."

And behold, there was in Jerusalem a man named Simeon, and this man was just and devout, looking for the consolation of Israel, and the Holy Spirit was upon him. And it had been revealed to him by the Holy Spirit that he should not see death before he had seen the Christ of the Lord. And he came by inspiration of the Spirit into the temple. And when his parents brought in the child Jesus, to do for him according to the custom of the Law, he also received him into his arms and blessed God, saying, "Now thou dost dismiss thy servant, O Lord, according to thy word, in peace; because my eyes have seen thy salvation, which thou hast prepared before the face of all peoples: a light of revelation to the Gentiles, and a glory for thy people Israel."

LUKE 2, 22-32

WASHINGTON, NATIONAL GALLERY OF ART   L'ORTOLANO,
(KRESS COLLECTION)   C.1488-1525

THE PRESENTATION IN THE TEMPLE

Queen of Patriarchs, Pray for Us

BUT when they had departed, behold, an angel of the Lord appeared in a dream to Joseph, saying, "Arise, and take the child and his mother, and flee into Egypt, and remain there until I tell thee. For Herod will seek the child to destroy him." So he arose, and took the child and his mother by night, and withdrew into Egypt, and remained there until the death of Herod; that what was spoken by the Lord through the prophet might be fulfilled, "Out of Egypt I called my son."

Then Herod, seeing that he had been tricked by the Magi, was exceedingly angry; and he sent and slew all the boys in Bethlehem and all its neighborhood who were two years old or under, according to the time that he had carefully ascertained from the Magi. Then was fulfilled what was spoken through Jeremias the prophet, "A voice was heard in Rama, weeping and loud lamentation; Rachel weeping for her children, and she would not be comforted, because they are no more."

But when Herod was dead, behold, an angel of the Lord appeared in a dream to Joseph in Egypt, saying, "Arise, and take the child and his mother, and go into the land of Israel, for those who sought the child's life are dead." So he arose and took the child and his mother, and went into the land of Israel.

MATTHEW 2, 13-21

ROME, VATICAN GALLERY   FEDERIGO BAROCCIO, 1528-1612

REST DURING THE FLIGHT
INTO EGYPT

Ark of the Covenant, Pray for Us

21

$\mathcal{A}$ND his parents were wont to go every year to Jerusalem at the Feast of the Passover. And when he was twelve years old, they went up to Jerusalem according to the custom of the feast. And after they had fulfilled the days, when they were returning, the boy Jesus remained in Jerusalem, and his parents did not know it. But thinking that he was in the caravan, they had come a day's journey before it occurred to them to look for him among their relatives and acquaintances. And not finding him, they returned to Jerusalem in search of him.

And it came to pass after three days, that they found him in the temple, sitting in the midst of the teachers, listening to them and asking them questions. And all who were listening to him were amazed at his understanding and his answers. And when they saw him, they were astonished. And his mother said to him, "Son, why hast thou done so to us? Behold, in sorrow thy father and I have been seeking thee."

And he said to them, "How is it that you sought me? Did you not know that I must be about my Father's business?" And they did not understand the word that he spoke to them.

And he went down with them and came to Nazareth, and was subject to them; and his mother kept all these things carefully in her heart. And Jesus advanced in wisdom and age and grace before God and men.

LUKE 2, 41-52

CHRIST AMONG THE DOCTORS

Tower of David, Pray for Us

". . . How did this man come by this wisdom and these miracles? Is not this the carpenter's son? Is not his mother called Mary . . . ?"

MATTHEW 13, 54-55

THE father of the just rejoiceth greatly: he that hath begotten a wise son, shall have joy in him. Let thy father and thy mother be joyful, and let her rejoice that bore thee.

PROVERBS 23, 24-25

O LORD Jesus Christ, Who by subjecting Thyself to Mary and Joseph didst consecrate family life with wonderful virtues: grant that, by their joint assistance, we may fashion our lives after the example of Thy Holy Family, and obtain everlasting fellowship with it.

PRAYER: MASS OF THE FEAST OF THE HOLY FAMILY

ROME, PRIVATE COLLECTION   DOMENICO MASTROIANNI, 1868-

IN JOSEPH'S SHOP

House of Gold, Pray for Us

ND on the third day a marriage took place at Cana of Galilee, and the mother of Jesus was there. Now Jesus too was invited to the marriage, and also his disciples. And the wine having run short, the mother of Jesus said to him, "They have no wine." And Jesus said to her, "What wouldst thou have me do, woman? My hour has not yet come." His mother said to the attendants, "Do whatever he tells you."

Now six stone water-jars were placed there, after the Jewish manner of purification, each holding two or three measures. Jesus said to them, "Fill the jars with water." And they filled them to the brim. And Jesus said to them, "Draw out now, and take to the chief steward." And they took it to him.

Now when the chief steward had tasted the water after it had become wine, not knowing whence it was (though the attendants who had drawn the water knew), the chief steward called the bridegroom, and said to him, "Every man at first sets forth the good wine, and when they have drunk freely, then that which is poorer. But thou hast kept the good wine until now."

This first of his signs Jesus worked at Cana of Galilee; and he manifested his glory, and his disciples believed in him. After this he went down to Capharnaum, he and his mother, and his brethren, and his disciples. And they stayed there but a few days.

JOHN 2, 1-12

PALESTINE, CHURCH OF CANA   FRANCOIS LE FOND, 1850-1900

THE MIRACLE AT CANA

Virgin Most Powerful, Pray for Us

AND bearing the cross for himself, he went forth to the place called the Skull, in Hebrew, Golgotha, where they crucified him . . .

JOHN 19, 17-18

NOW there were standing by the cross of Jesus his mother and his mother's sister, Mary of Cleophas, and Mary Magdalene. When Jesus, therefore, saw his mother and the disciple standing by, whom he loved, he said to his mother, "Woman, behold, thy son." Then he said to the disciple, "Behold, thy mother." And from that hour the disciple took her into his home.

JOHN 19, 25-27

IT was now about the sixth hour, and there was darkness over the whole land until the ninth hour. And the sun was darkened, and the curtain of the temple was torn in the middle. And Jesus cried out with a loud voice and said, "Father, into thy hands I commend my spirit." And having said this, he expired.

LUKE 23, 44-46

THE CRUCIFIXION

Queen of Martyrs, Pray for Us

ND behold, there was a man named Joseph, a councillor, a good and just man—he had not been party to their plan of action—of Arimathea, a town of Judea, who was himself looking for the kingdom of God. He went to Pilate and asked for the body of Jesus.

And he took him down, and wrapped him in a linen cloth, and laid him in a rock-hewn tomb where no one had ever yet been laid. And it was Preparation Day, and the Sabbath was drawing on. And the women who had come with him from Galilee, followed after, and beheld the tomb, and how his body was laid. And they went back and prepared spices and ointments. And on the Sabbath they rested, in accordance with the commandment.

LUKE 23, 50-56

HEY therefore took the body of Jesus and wrapped it in linen cloths with the spices, after the Jewish manner of preparing for burial. Now in the place where he was crucified there was a garden, and in the garden a new tomb in which no one had yet been laid. There, accordingly, because of the Preparation Day of the Jews, for the tomb was close at hand, they laid Jesus.

JOHN 19, 40-42

THE DESCENT FROM THE CROSS

Comforter of the Afflicted, Pray for Us

ᴮUT on the first day of the week at early dawn, they came to the tomb, taking the spices that they had prepared, and they found the stone rolled back from the tomb. But on entering, they did not find the body of the Lord Jesus. And it came to pass, while they were wondering what to make of this, that, behold, two men stood by them in dazzling raiment. And when the women were struck with fear and bowed their faces to the ground, they said to them, "Why do you seek the living one among the dead? He is not here, but has risen. Remember how he spoke to you while he was yet in Galilee, saying that the Son of Man must be betrayed into the hands of sinful men, and be crucified, and on the third day rise."

LUKE 24, 1-7

ᴵ AROSE, and am still with Thee, alleluia: Thou hast laid Thy hand upon Me, alleluia; Thy knowledge is become wonderful, alleluia, alleluia.

INTROIT: MASS OF THE FEAST OF THE RESURRECTION

O GOD, Who on this day, through Thy Only-begotten Son, didst overcome death, and open unto us the gate of everlasting Life: as, by Thy antici-pating grace, Thou dost breathe good desires into our hearts, so also, by Thy gracious help, bring them to good effect.

PRAYER: MASS OF THE FEAST OF THE RESURRECTION

FLORENCE, MUSEUM SAN MARCO   FRA ANGELICO, 1387-1455

THE RESURRECTION

Queen of Peace, Pray for Us

33

So then the Lord, after he had spoken to them, was taken up into heaven, and sits at the right hand of God.

MARK 16, 19

. . . HE was lifted up before their eyes, and a cloud took him out of their sight. And . . . behold, two men stood by them in white garments, and said to them, "Men of Galilee, why do you stand looking up to heaven? This Jesus who has been taken up from you into heaven, shall come in the same way as you have seen him going up to heaven."

ACTS 1, 9-11

Now he led them out towards Bethany, and he lifted up his hands and blessed them. And it came to pass as he blessed them, that he parted from them and was carried up into heaven. And they worshipped him, and returned to Jerusalem with great joy. And they were continually in the temple, praising and blessing God.

LUKE 24, 50-53

GRANT, we beseech Thee, almighty God, that we who believe Thine Only-begotten Son, our Redeemer, to have this day ascended into heaven, may ourselves also in mind dwell amid heavenly things.

PRAYER: MASS OF THE FEAST OF THE ASCENSION

PADUA, SCROVEGNI CHAPEL   GIOTTO DI BONDONE, 1276?-1337

THE ASCENSION

Gate of Heaven, Pray for Us

35

ND when the days of Pentecost were drawing to a close, they were all together in one place. And suddenly there came a sound from heaven, as of a violent wind blowing, and it filled the whole house where they were sitting. And there appeared to them parted tongues as of fire, which settled upon each of them. And they were all filled with the Holy Spirit and began to speak in foreign tongues, even as the Holy Spirit prompted them to speak.

Now there were staying at Jerusalem devout Jews from every nation under heaven. And when this sound was heard, the multitude gathered and were bewildered in mind, because each heard them speaking in his own language. But they were all amazed and marvelled, saying, "Behold, are not all these that are speaking Galileans?"

ACTS 2, 1-7

O GOD, Who on this day by the light of the Holy Spirit didst teach the hearts of the faithful, grant us by the same Spirit to relish what is right, and always to rejoice in His comfort.

PRAYER: MASS OF THE FEAST OF PENTECOST

MAY the inpouring of the Holy Spirit cleanse our hearts, O Lord, and render them fertile by the inward sprinkling of His heavenly dew.

POSTCOMMUNION: MASS OF THE FEAST OF PENTECOST

ROME, PALLOTTINE SEMINARY   GREGORY MALTZEFF, 1881-1953

PENTECOST

Queen of Apostles, Pray for Us

37

$\mathcal{A}$ND a great sign appeared in heaven: a woman clothed with the sun, and the moon was under her feet, and upon her head a crown of twelve stars.

APOCALYPSE 12, 1

$\mathcal{T}$HE Lord has blessed thee by His power, because by thee He has brought our enemies to naught. Blessed are thou, O daughter, by the Lord the most high God, above all women upon the earth. Blessed be the Lord Who made heaven and earth, Who has directed thee to the cutting off the head of the prince of our enemies, because He has so magnified thy name this day, that thy praise shall not depart out of the mouth of men who shall be mindful of the power of the Lord forever; for that thou hast not spared thy life, by reason of the distress and tribulation of thy people, but hast prevented our ruin in the presence of our God. Thou art the glory of Jerusalem, thou art the joy of Israel, thou art the honor of our people.

EPISTLE: MASS OF THE FEAST OF THE ASSUMPTION OF
THE BLESSED VIRGIN MARY

ROME, DORIAN GALLERY   ANIBALE CARRACCI, 1560-1609

THE ASSUMPTION OF THE VIRGIN

Queen of Angels, Pray for Us

39

ℏAIL, Holy Queen, Mother of Mercy, our life, our sweetness, and our hope! To thee do we cry, poor banished children of Eve; to thee do we send up our sighs, mourning and weeping in this valley of tears. Turn then, most gracious advocate, thine eyes of mercy towards us; and after this our exile, show unto us the blessed fruit of thy womb, Jesus. O clement, O loving, O sweet Virgin Mary.

SALVE REGINA

O ALMIGHTY and eternal God, Who didst assume unto celestial glory, in body and soul, the Immaculate Virgin Mary, the Mother of Thy Son, grant we beseech Thee, that ever intent on heavenly things, we may be worthy to share in her glory.

PRAYER: MASS OF THE FEAST OF THE ASSUMPTION OF
THE BLESSED VIRGIN MARY

MOTHER of Christ! hear thou thy people's cry, Star of the deep, and Portal of the sky! Mother of Him who thee from nothing made, sinking we strive, and call to thee for aid: Oh, by that joy which Gabriel brought to thee, thou Virgin first and last, let us thy mercy see.

ALMA REDEMPTORIS MATER

THE CORONATION OF THE VIRGIN

Queen of All Saints, Pray for Us

41

FORMERLY IN THE DRESDEN ART GALLERY   RAPHAEL SANZIO,
1483-1520

THE SISTINE MADONNA

Mother Most Admirable, Pray for Us

For nearly two thousand years veneration of the Madonna has been an inspiration and vital force in the Christian world. Her influence has proved a profound and humanizing factor in the development of painting throughout the centuries, and the part that the Catholic Church has played in this period as "the first and foremost patron of the arts" cannot be stressed too strongly.

The great masterpieces depicting Our Lady are eloquent proof of the part she plays in inspiring artistic genius. Tender, compassionate and self-effacing, Mary is regarded as the ideal symbol of Motherhood, and it is natural that each race and nation should regard her as its very own.

The more significant events in the life of Our Lady have been presented with appropriate text. In the following pages, as many different conceptions of Mary, Queen of the Universe, are included as space permits. The famous paintings reproduced have one thing in common; all are positive proof of the Virgin's secure hold on the hearts of men and of her ability to arouse the deepest religious sentiments in mankind.

We may all take pride in the knowledge that these works of art are part of our heritage and that through them we may seek to discover the beneficence and power, the purity, humility and love of MARY— God's Masterpiece.

HEAD OF THE
VIRGIN (detail)
SANDRO BOTTICELLI,
1444?-1510
BERLIN,
KAISER FRIEDRICH MUSEUM

VIRGIN AND CHILD
CESARE DA SESTO,
1477-1527
MILAN,
BRERA GALLERY

HEAD OF THE
VIRGIN (detail)
BERNARDINO LUINI,
C.1475-1532
MILAN,
BRERA GALLERY

THE HOLY FAMILY

PETER PAUL RUBENS,
1577-1640

FLORENCE,
PITTI GALLERY

45

THE MADONNA OF
THE ROSE BED
(detail)
FRANCESCO FRANCIA,
1450?-1517
MUNICH,
ALTE GALLERY

THE VIRGIN OF
THE ROCKS
LEONARDO DA VINCI,
1452-1519
PARIS,
THE LOUVRE

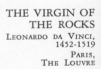

46

MADONNA AND
CHILD
ANDREA DEL VERROCCHIO,
1435-1488
BERLIN,
KAISER FRIEDRICH MUSEUM

THE MADONNA OF
THE POPLARS
GIOVANNI BELLINI,
1430?-1516
VENICE,
ACADEMY OF FINE ARTS

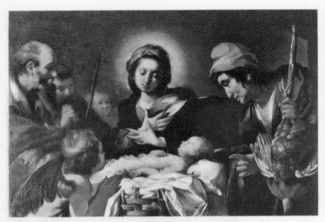

THE ADORATION OF THE SHEPHERDS
BERNARDO STROZZI, 1581-1644
BALTIMORE, WALTERS ART GALLERY

HEAD OF THE
VIRGIN (detail)
PIETRO PERUGINO,
1445-1523
FLORENCE,
UFFIZI GALLERY

48

THE ADORATION OF THE MAGI
ALESSANDRO TIARINI, 1577-1668
ROME, CORSINI GALLERY

HEAD OF THE
VIRGIN (detail)
DOMENICO GHIRLANDAIO,
1449-1494
FLORENCE,
FOUNDLING HOSPITAL

49

THE ADORATION OF THE MAGI
SEBASTIANO CONCA, 1679-1764
ROME, CORSINI GALLERY

REST ON THE FLIGHT INTO EGYPT
ANTHONY VAN DYKE, 1599-1641
FLORENCE, PITTI GALLERY

MADONNA AND CHILD (detail)
ANTONIO CORREGGIO, 1494-1534
PARMA, PICTURE GALLERY

THE VIRGIN AND CHILD WITH ANGELS
CARLO MARATTI, 1625-1713
ROME, CORSINI GALLERY

51

THE MADONNA OF
THE GRAND DUKE
Raphael Sanzio,
1483-1520
Florence,
Pitti Gallery

THE HOLY FAMILY
Carlo Maratti,
1625-1713
Rome,
Vatican Gallery

THE HOLY FAMILY

El Greco,
c.1545-1614

Cleveland,
Museum of Art

THE VIRGIN OF
THE CHAPLET

Bartolomé Murillo,
1617-1682

Florence,
Pitti Gallery

53

THE VIRGIN IN
ADORATION
(detail)
FRA FILIPPO LIPPI,
1406?-1469
FLORENCE,
UFFIZI GALLERY

MADONNA AND
CHILD
PINTORICCHIO,
1454-1513
ROME,
VATICAN GALLERY

THE VIRGIN IN
ADORATION
(detail)
FRANCESCO BOTTICINI,
1446-1498
VENICE,
CA' D'ORO

THE MADONNA OF
THE CARNATION
BERNARDINO LUINI,
C.1475-1532
WASHINGTON,
NATIONAL GALLERY OF ART
(KRESS COLLECTION)

55

MADONNA AND
CHILD
Il Sassoferrato,
1605-1685
Milan,
Brera Gallery

MADONNA AND
CHILD
Pompeo Batoni,
1708-1787
Rome,
Borghese Gallery

HEAD OF THE
MADONNA
CARLO DOLCI,
1616-1686
TURIN,
REALE GALLERY

THE MADONNA OF
THE CROWN
AMBROGIO BORGOGNONE,
c. 1450-1523
MILAN,
BRERA GALLERY

57

THE MADONNA OF
THE HARPIES
Andrea del Sarto,
1486-1531
Florence,
Uffizi Gallery

THE MADONNA
AND CHILD IN
THE CHURCH
Jan van Eyck,
1370?-1440?
Berlin,
Kaiser Friedrich Museum

THE VIRGIN IN
PRAYER
ALBRECHT DÜRER,
1471-1528
BERLIN,
KAISER FRIEDRICH MUSEUM

MADONNA AND
CHILD
HANS MEMLING,
c.1430-1494
BERLIN,
KAISER FRIEDRICH MUSEUM

THE REST ON THE
FLIGHT INTO EGYPT
GERARD DAVID,
c.1460-1523
WASHINGTON,
NATIONAL GALLERY OF ART
(MELLON COLLECTION)

THE HOLY FAMILY
WITH ST. CATHERINE
JOSÉ DE RIBERA,
1591-1652
NEW YORK,
METROPOLITAN MUSEUM

THE VIRGIN OF THE GRAPES

THE HOLY FAMILY

61

THE LITTLE MADONNA

ROBERTO FERRUZZI,
1854-?

FLORENCE,
PRIVATE COLLECTION

VIRGIN, INFANT
AND ST. JOHN

SANDRO BOTTICELLI,
1444?-1510

PARIS,
THE LOUVRE

THE MADONNA OF
THE OLIVES
Nicolo Barabino,
1832-1891
Sampierdarena Cathedral

THE NATIVITY
Gian Pittoni,
1687-1767
Rovigo,
Concord Gallery

VIRGIN AND CHILD

Domenico Morelli,
1826-1901

Rome,
Scaletta Collection

OUR LADY OF
MOTHER LOVE

C. Bosseron Chambers,
Contemporary

Washington,
Franciscan Monastery

Index of Artists